Romaine Morgan

World Of Digital Marketing

Learning The Fundamentals Of Digital Marketing

Romaine Morgan

Book by Romaine Morgan

Romaine Morgan

Romaine Morgan

Romaine Morgan

Table of contents

- OPENING -

Digital marketing is a game-changer in today's global marketplace, which is always changing and evolving. Learning digital marketing is not an option if you want to climb the corporate ladder to new heights and make a name for yourself in today's cutthroat industry; it's a must.

The globe is more linked than ever before, and a large percentage of the population lives online. Everything that matters, from researching a product to making a purchase, takes place in the digital realm. The secret to unimaginable prospects awaits the astute professional who knows how to tap into this vast internet potential. The unstoppable force that may take your personal or company's brand to new heights is digital marketing. Let us begin by discussing the immense scope of digital marketing. You can reach a huge and varied audience through digital marketing because most people on the planet use the internet.

Imagine a world where potential clients can be reached effortlessly, regardless of their location, with just a single click. With the help of digital marketing, your skills or wares might be seen by a large and interested audience all over the world. Its low price tag is a major selling point for digital marketing. It can be difficult for individuals or small enterprises to compete with larger organizations when using traditional marketing methods due to the high costs associated with them. But things are different in the digital sphere.

You can build effective campaigns on a budget with the help of techniques like content marketing, search engine optimization, and social media advertising. Entrepreneurs and driven professionals may now increase their impact and reach a wider audience without breaking the bank, thanks to the democratization of marketing. The instantaneous nature of digital advertising is something we should discuss now.

Time is of the essence in today's fast-paced society. Digital marketing is lightning fast compared to traditional marketing strategies, which might take weeks or months to produce results. Would you like to begin a particular campaign tomorrow? That is not only doable, but also incredibly efficient, with digital marketing. One advantage over more conventional approaches is the capacity to change course quickly in reaction to emerging patterns and data.

Reaching the correct people is more important than reaching a large audience when it comes to digital marketing. Reaching the people most likely to interact with your business is possible with the help of sophisticated targeting tools that allow you to personalize your communications based on demographics, hobbies, and behaviors. This degree of specificity not only reduces the likelihood of wasting dollars on unconverted groups but also increases the effectiveness of your marketing campaigns.

Having a one-on-one chat with every prospective client is like bridging the digital barrier with an authentic interaction. Data plays an essential part in digital marketing and should not be overlooked. In the digital world, every interaction—like, click, and share—creates a mountain of data. This information is more than simply raw statistics; it provides a practical understanding of customer habits, tastes, and tendencies.

Your strategies, campaigns, and decision-making may be fine-tuned, optimized, and result-driven with the help of analytics. Information is now worth more than ever before, and digital marketers are the astute financiers that can make the most of this trend. Last but not least, my esteemed audience, we must adapt to a changing environment.

Learning digital marketing is more than just acquiring new skills; it's a game-changer that can alter the course of your career. If you want to be successful in today's competitive job market, whether you're an established professional, an aspiring entrepreneur, or anything in between, learning digital marketing is a must.

Digital marketing is your ticket to financial success in today's online economy. You may take advantage of this chance, join the digital revolution, and see your professional or personal brand reach new heights if you do. Individuals with influence in digital marketing are shaping a digital future.

Romaine Morgan

- CHAPTER I -
INTRO TO DIGITAL MARKETING

Digital marketing has become the unrivaled leader in promoting brands and engaging customers in today's lightning-fast commercial environment. It is the hidden ingredient that turns average companies into digital dynasties —the very essence of contemporary trade.

In this enthralling exploration, we will follow the lead of a seasoned seller who is ready to demonstrate the transformative power of digital marketing by delving into its definition and history. Digital Marketing: A Precise Definition Essentially, digital marketing is all about connecting with your target audience where

they spend the majority of their time—online.
It's not limited to just one platform; rather, it's
an ever-changing ecosystem that includes a
plethora of channels like websites, social
media, and search engines.

Engaging content meets data-driven insights
to create an irresistible appeal for the target
audience through the strategic combination of
creativity and technology. Think of it this way: a
virtual storefront that is open all the time,
anywhere in the world, to prospective buyers.
The beauty of internet marketing is that your
brand's offers are always on display, waiting to
fascinate and convert.

In digital marketing, everything from eye-
catching Instagram ads to well-planned email
campaigns and search engine optimization-
savvy websites comes together to tell a

brand's story. Here we go again to see how digital marketing has progressed over the years —a path characterized by change, innovation, and the never-ending quest for excellence. Banner advertisements and pop-ups dominated the early days of the Internet, when marketers battled for visibility in the disorganized space of the Internet.

However, marketers also grew more savvy as customers did. Brands were thrust to the forefront of search engine results during the era of pay-per-click (PPC) advertising and search engine optimization (SEO). It went from being there to claiming the top slot, which ensures visibility and clicks, all of a sudden. As a means of manipulating search engine ranks, digital marketers essentially became algorithm designers. The next exciting development in this compelling story was the rise of social media. Social media sites like Instagram, Twitter, and Facebook became online marketplaces where firms could have live discussions, establish communities, and show off their personalities instead of just having a website.

As digital marketing shifted from transactional to relationship-based, influential people became the natural and engaging spokespersons for brands, amplifying their messages with style and authenticity. Once thought to be an anachronism, email marketing has recently made a triumphant return as a potent tool for targeted outreach. By using automation techniques, targeted campaigns were made possible, allowing for the timely delivery of the right message to the right audience. Digital marketers evolved into conductors, composing symphonies of consumer journeys that spoke to each person's unique tastes and habits. In the age of data analytics and AI, however, each action— from clicking to scrolling to hovering—became an important component.

In order to develop tactics and anticipate consumer trends, digital marketers now depend on data-driven insights, moving beyond guessing. Instant, individualized experiences for customers were made possible by the proliferation of chatbots and virtual assistants, further blurring the boundaries between human connection and automation. The merging of imagination and technology has brought us to the peak of digital marketing's development. Immersive experiences are the new money; storytelling is king; and video content is king. With the advent of AR and VR, companies now have the chance to take customers to other worlds where their items appear in extraordinary detail. To sum up, digital marketing is more than a tool; it's a powerful force that has transformed the way brands engage with customers.

This transformation has been nothing short of remarkable, starting with the relatively simple banner advertisements and ending with today's fully immersive experiences. As an experienced digital salesperson, I urge you to take advantage of this revolutionary power, to tap into the possibilities of pixels and algorithms, and to take your brand to new heights. Welcome to the golden age of digital marketing, where the adventure is exciting and the possibilities are endless! Digital marketing is the key thread in the complex web of today's corporate environment, connecting dots, raising brand awareness, and energizing the commercial process.

Businesses rely on it to stay up-to-date with the constantly changing trends in customer behavior and technical improvements; its significance goes beyond just advertising. As we explore the intricate details of the digital marketing landscape, it becomes clear that its importance lies not only in the swiftness of its effects but also in the radical transformation of modern company tactics. The power of digital marketing to bypass time and space limitations is fundamental to its relevance. Any company, no matter how big or small, can reach customers all over the world in the digital arena, which acts as a borderless agora. Online storefronts, which exhibit items and services to potential clients all day, every day, eliminate the limits of traditional brick-and-mortar companies.

Digital marketing plays a key role in today's market, spreading the word about a brand's infinitely scalable qualities around the clock. Digital marketing acts as a watchful navigator in the consumer behavior mosaic, picking up on small cues and quickly adjusting to the ever-changing tastes of an ever-changing audience. The contemporary customer is an integral part of the story of brand engagement, rather than just an observer. Digital marketing creates an immersive experience that speaks to each consumer's uniqueness through personalized content, social media platforms, and search engines that facilitate a responsive and engaging discussion. One of digital marketing's most important functions is leveling the playing field so that small and medium-sized enterprises (SMEs) can compete with larger ones. In the past, smaller businesses often felt they had little say in the matter due to the high costs associated with establishing a brand's visibility in the market.

But there is an inexpensive way to get your name out there: digital marketing. Businesses of all sizes may carve out a niche using easily accessible channels such as social media campaigns, SEO, and email marketing. Moreover, digital marketing is more than just a platform for promotional messaging; it allows organizations to gain data-driven insights that help them fine-tune and customize their plans with accuracy. Analytics shed light on complex patterns of customer behavior, preferences, and interactions, putting an end to the age of guessing. Data allows companies to see how well their campaigns are doing, learn about their audience's demographics, and adjust their strategies in real-time, allowing them to be more agile strategically than before.

Digital marketing has emerged as a master storyteller in this age of short attention spans and intense rivalry for visibility. Brands build resonance with their audience through content, which can take many forms, such as appealing blog posts, engaging social media videos, or email newsletters. Digital marketing goes beyond simple product sales by creating emotional connections with customers through well-crafted narratives. This results in brand supporters who see brands as more than just sellers; they are curators of meaningful experiences. The shift from brick-and-mortar stores to online platforms has highlighted the critical role of digital marketing in molding consumers' opinions of brands.

Customers often interact with a company for the first time through its digital presence, and their impressions of the business are heavily influenced by the quality of the user experience they have. To create a lasting impression and establish a basis for customer connections, it is important to have responsive websites, user-friendly interfaces, and easy navigation. Finally, digital marketing is not an afterthought in today's corporate world; rather, it is the hero of a story about change and adaptability. It has an impact on everything from consumer acquisition to brand loyalty, and it's not limited to the digital sphere. In my role as a writer following this story, I've noticed how digital marketing is shaping up to be more than simply a tool; it's the foundation of modern commerce, a proof that adaptation is essential in the dynamic dance of economics.

Navigating the maze of digital marketing platforms is like conducting a symphony of strategic melodies in an ever-growing and expansive world. In the orchestration of brand exposure and interaction, every channel plays an individual role. Join me on a literary journey as I unravel the enthralling tales told by four crucial digital marketing channels: search engine optimization (SEO), search engine marketing (SEM), social media, and email marketing. Optimizing Your Website for Search

Engines: A Magical Process for More Views Search Engine Optimization (SEO) is the magical formula for visibility in the otherworldly domain of search engines, where algorithms control the rise and fall of digital tides. SEO, or search engine optimization, is, at its core, the practice of crafting web content in such a way that it appeals to both humans and search engines' algorithmic judgment.

When done well, the combination of keywords, meta tags, and high-quality content may catapult a brand to the top of search engine results pages. Search engine optimization is like a silent conductor arranging the notes of organic traffic. In an online environment where people believe in organic search results, search engine optimization (SEO) creates a story that makes a company seem like an invited guest rather than an invasive outsider. Search engine optimization (SEO) makes sure that a brand's message reverberates throughout the whole internet, resonating in the halls of user intent and curiosity, by means of on-page optimization, off-page tactics, and the everlasting pursuit of relevance.

The Master of Accuracy: Search engine marketing (SEM) While search engine optimization (SEO) is like a painter's brushstrokes, search engine marketing (SEM) is like a conductor with a baton full of precision. Search engine marketing (SEM) includes all of the paid tactics that get brands to the top of the SERPs. Paid search advertising, sponsored listings, and strategic bidding are all parts of search engine marketing (SEM), which builds visibility beyond what organic search can do on its own. Search engine optimization (SEO) makes sure that businesses resonate in the ever-changing digital advertising landscape, where each click contributes to the overall user engagement.

It is the platform where companies can compete for prominent placement in the online marketplace, where people are looking for answers to their questions. Search engine marketing (SEM) is the lifeblood of brand exposure, resonating in the world of immediate visibility and strategic prominence with its data-driven insights and immediate impact. Engaging with Social Media: A Multi-Factor Maze Welcome to the colorful world of social media, a rich tapestry where businesses take center stage as storytellers and customers play an active role as co-narrators. In order to go beyond simple transactional involvement and really connect with consumers, businesses are turning to social media marketing.

Brands express themselves, interact with consumers, and build communities outside of the realm of conventional advertising on social media sites such as LinkedIn, Facebook, Twitter, and Instagram. When it comes to capturing attention in a world where thumb-scroll rules, social media is the avant-garde artist, using graphics, films, and captivating storylines.

It's about encouraging dialogue rather than just broadcasting messages. Brand tales are propelled into collective awareness by viral content, which turns hashtags into rallying cries. The instantaneity and genuineness of social media marketing give new life to the concept of corporate identity by making corporations feel more like people.

Email marketing stands out in this day of overloaded inboxes, providing a personalized connection through its tiny symphony of chords. It is the pathway that bypasses the din of digital chaos and reaches people where they spend the most time: in the privacy of their own homes. Marketing via email is not a bomb; rather, it is a nuanced orchestration of tailored promotions, informative information, and personalized communications that aims to appeal to each recipient's unique tastes.

Email marketing creates a harmonious whole that includes lead nurturing and customer retention via segmentation, automation, and an acute awareness of the customer journey. As a reliable travel companion on the web, it is the channel that contacts customers about abandoned carts, greets them with personalized suggestions, and offers them exclusive invitations. The inbox goes from being a boring container to a captivating stage for captivating narratives, thanks to the eloquence of email marketing.

At the end of the day, the digital marketing world is like a complex sonnet, with each channel playing an important role in the overall story of how people see and interact with brands. Online marketing is a complex web that includes search engine optimization (SEO), search engine marketing (SEM), social media marketing (SMM), and email marketing (EM). Artistic elements, literary methods, and musical notes all come together to form a harmonious whole that echoes the beat of the modern digital age.

Romaine Morgan

- CHAPTER 2 -
UNDERSTANDING YOUR AUDIENCE

With the deft touch of a master craftsman, marketing maestros know that precisely identifying their target demographic and crafting consumer personas constitute the beating heart of their campaigns. In copywriting, words are more than simply letters; they are the building blocks of an engaging story with the power to persuade. The true magic happens when we define our target audiences and create buyer personas. Let's get there together.

Achieving Harmony with Your Audience: The Symphony of the Target Audience Knowing your audience inside and out is like the conductor's baton in a marketing symphony. Finding an audience that fits your brand like a glove is more important than simply reaching an audience at large. Picture this in your mind: you're in the business of selling exotic sports cars with top-tier performance.

Imagine yourself at the wheel of your ideal convertible, listening to the sound of the engine revving and the wind in your hair. Who would it be? This vivid picture is what you need to define your target audience. Are these wealthy people looking for the pinnacle of luxury, or are they young professionals who value speed and style?

This fundamental comprehension is the bedrock upon which you build your copy's language, channels, and emotional evocation.

Accuracy is paramount in the vast marketing tapestry. To catch that elusive fish, you need to cast a net with the ideal mesh, not merely a wide net, and hope for the best. Allow me to introduce you to the personal realm of buyer personas. Think of your ideal customers as the heroes of a great tale, and your buyer personas as the supporting cast.

Rather than being cold, hard numbers, these personas are actual people with hopes, dreams, fears, and other human emotions. Introducing Alex, a Pioneer in Technology: Someone who is young, tech-savvy, and constantly seeking out new devices Your product seems like it could be the starting point for Alex's aspiration to be an innovator. Next, we have Olivia, the Environmental Heroine: Concerned about her impact on the environment, she is deeply committed to sustainability. For her, buying your goods is more than just a transaction; it's an act of activism toward a more sustainable world. You can tailor your approach and weave a story that speaks directly to your audience's hopes and goals by developing these buyer personas. What you write is more than simply words on a page; it's an interaction with real people, each of whom has a story to tell.

Where Buyer Personas and Target Audiences Meet: The Alchemy of Connection Let your buyer personas tell a story based on real people, and harmonize your target audience's demographics. In this magical union, your text becomes more than just words; it becomes an irresistible magnet that pulls readers in. Consider your ideal customers as the endpoint and your buyer personas as the means by which they will reach your target market. You are the guideposts, the beautiful scenery, and the adventurers in your copy.

It's more than just making a sale; it's about taking your customers on an emotional journey that speaks to their souls. The secret ingredient is writing copy that resonates deeply with your target audience's buyer personas. What makes Alex's eyes light up with delight are the keywords; therefore, it's important to learn his language. Making environmentally conscious claims that are in line with Olivia's objective is all about connecting with her ideals. Your text transforms from an advertising tool into a trusted friend and guide at this point of confluence. Not only does it make a sale, but it also strikes a chord with the target demographic and makes a lasting impression on them.

Refining and Iterating: The Last Flourish The process as a copywriter doesn't finish with a well-written piece; it just starts. Audiences and personas change as the market does. The art of refining and iterating is where it all comes together. Hear the murmurs of others who will be watching you. Be on the lookout for changes in their tastes and goals.

Move with the grace of a dancer whose steps change in time with the music. The capacity to change and adapt is what gives your copy its life and strength. Finally, the foundation of effective copywriting is identifying target audiences and creating buyer personas. It's the magical ingredient that turns your speech into an emotional masterpiece that stays with your listeners long after the last note has faded. So channel your inner genius and watch the magic happen as you use your words. Market research is a powerful weapon for the astute entrepreneur in the complex dance of business, where fortunes surge and fall like waves.

Think of it as a compass that guides a ship across the treacherous waters of shifting customer tastes, market tendencies, and rivalry. Learning the ins and outs of market research is the first step toward a prosperous path. Decisions made by businesses are based on market research.

To analyze the market and find trends that can determine a company's fate is more than just collecting data; it's a strategic activity. Demarcating the boundaries is the initial stroke of this deft brush. In your opinion, which questions require answers? In developing a new product, are you venturing into unexplored territory or are you honing an existing one? A well-defined goal is the foundation of an efficient and effective research campaign. In the vast tapestry of corporate strategy, market research assumes many shapes and sizes, each of which is essential yet distinct.

Think of quantitative research as a bird's-eye perspective of the market and all the numbers and trends in it. Using this approach—whether via analytics, polls, or surveys—provides decision-makers with a statistical picture that is empirically precise. Now, like a painter examining a painting's finer points, conduct qualitative research by zooming in.

Numerical analyses miss subtleties that can be better understood by in-depth interviews, focus groups, and conversations. The statistical framework would be nothing without the qualitative data that gives the market its meat and potatoes. When these methods are combined, they form a potent synergy that provides a holistic perspective of the market that goes beyond simple observation. Knowing "what" isn't enough; you also need to grasp "why" and "how." Consumers play the role of conductors in the commercial symphony, with their demands serving as the musical notes. Being a good listener is an art form in market research.

Think about a smartphone company that does market research. Which characteristics are most desired by customers? Is it the state-of-the-art camera equipment, the blazing fast processor, or the stylish design? Companies can create a product that perfectly suits their target market's needs by keeping tabs on customer tastes. Gaining insight into client requirements is an ongoing process. The conversation is ever-changing, reflecting the rhythm of the market. Businesses can keep in sync with the ever-changing notes of consumer expectations by regularly conducting market research and adjusting and organizing their offers accordingly.

Everyone is a sailor in the market, and everyone is trying to catch the same wind of success. When it comes to this, market research is like a spyglass; it lets companies see what their competitors are up to. Imagine a busy neighborhood that is about to welcome a new coffee shop. The company can learn about the current coffee shops' advantages and disadvantages, as well as their own distinct selling factors, by doing a competitive analysis. Instead of trying to imitate your competitors, you should plot a course that takes advantage of unfulfilled consumer requirements and gaps in the market.

This understanding is priceless, like a seasoned navigator looking over previous paths before deciding on one. Businesses may avoid dangerous seas and take advantage of unrealized possibilities by having a clear picture of the competitive landscape. In the ever-changing world of business, trends are like ebb and flow: they can lift a company to new heights or sink it to oblivion.

Predicting the ebb and flow of trends before they become tsunamis requires a keen eye, and market research provides just that. Just look at the internet industry and how quickly trends can change, much like sand dunes in the wind. Emerging technology, shifting customer tastes, and cultural shifts can all be identified through market research. With this insight, they can ride the wave of innovation, leading the pack and making sure their products and services are always in demand. Market research is more than a window into the here and now; it's a window into the future. Successful companies aren't reactive but rather proactive in their approach to the market.

It takes a mix of intellectual skill and gut feeling to predict future trends. To do this, one must be able to extrapolate from available data, spot new trends, and predict where the market will go. Taking a proactive stance allows companies to be at the forefront instead of just following the crowd, allowing them to grab opportunities before they ever happen. Instead of a massive study collecting dust, market research should lead to an insight that motivates strategic action. When insights are turned into practical tactics, they can propel a firm to great heights. Suppose a clothing store finds out through surveys that eco-friendly clothing is trending.

There is a call to action included in this revelation; it is more than just information. The store is compelled to change its procurement methods, use more environmentally friendly items, and show their dedication to sustainability. They are appealing to a rising demographic of eco-conscious shoppers while simultaneously staying in step with current market trends. If you're embarking on a company journey, market research isn't a side trip; it's an essential component. What separates a ship aimlessly drifting through turbulent waves from one plotting a precise course is this: Doing business without first conducting thorough market research is like trying to navigate a storm without a map or compass.

Those that fully commit to its methodology, however, will find market research to be an invaluable tool, guiding them towards well-informed judgments, strategic positioning, and long-term success. With market research at their disposal, navigators are more than simply sailor-men in the treacherous commercial seas; they are masters of their own fate. In this digital world, where every activity has an electronic footprint, data analytics is a powerful tool in the hands of the astute marketer. Picture it as a highly tuned radar system, scanning the enormous landscape of user behavior to reveal the hidden preferences, habits, and aspirations of the audience. Data analytics is like the conductor of a marketing symphony; it brings together disparate insights in a way that makes everything crystal clear. Data analytics boils down to mastering the complex web of audience behavior.

A digital footprint is left behind by every online contact, whether it's visiting a website or engaging with social media. Skilled analysts use algorithms and tools to piece together these pieces and paint a complete picture of the audience's behavior. Just imagine an e-commerce platform that tracks how customers use their site. You may learn a lot about what customers are interested in, the steps they take before buying, and what causes them to leave their carts empty by analyzing data. A better user experience, more personalized services, and higher conversion rates are all possible with this kind of detailed insight into audience behavior.

Data analytics goes beyond simple statistics by creating comprehensive profiles of target audiences. Understanding why a person clicked on a particular product is more important than simply knowing that they did so. Marketers can learn more about consumers' demographics, tastes, and even psychographics by using data analytics. Picture this: a streaming service that provides entertainment and analyzes user data. Data analytics not only reveals a viewer's viewing patterns but also their age, location, genre preferences, and viewing periods. With this detailed profile in hand, the service may compile recommendations just for you, deliver targeted promotions to certain demographics, and adjust the content strategy to suit your tastes. Data analytics has a little bit of magical predicting power; it's not just for solving mysteries.

Analytics acts like a crystal ball by revealing trends and patterns in past data, allowing us to see how audiences will behave in the future. Think about a subscription-based company that uses data analytics to predict customer turnover. They can detect warning signs and take preventative actions to keep consumers by looking at historical user behavior that led to subscription cancellations. With the use of predictive analytics, companies can turn uncertainty into foresight and meet customer demands before they even think about them. No two audiences are ever the same in the kaleidoscope of human variation. Here we employ segmentation, the data analytics magic bullet. Marketers are able to deploy strategies with pinpoint accuracy when they divide consumers into subsets defined by commonalities in traits, habits, or interests. Imagine a campaign that promotes a new fitness app through email.

Data analytics divides the target demographic into three groups: fitness aficionados, newbies, and people looking to achieve particular health objectives. A tailored message that speaks to the specific wants and desires of each group is sent out. By using this segmentation magic, marketers can make their ads more effective and more relatable to different demographics. Data analytics' real-time capabilities are its crowning glory. It's the conductor's baton that ties together a symphony of responsive marketing strategies; it's more than just a tool for retrospective analysis.

Data analytics guarantees that marketing campaigns stay up with the lightning-fast pace of the digital arena. Think about a social media marketing campaign that tracks engagement data in real-time. Using data analytics as a guide, a smart marketer will grab the opportunity if content unexpectedly does well with a specific audience segment. They make instantaneous adjustments to the campaign's direction, focusing on what works and boosting the parts that get results. Data analytics keeps this reactivity robust and consistent, which is the current marketing rhythm.

The end game for many companies is conversion, or the process of changing prospects into paying customers. Businesses rely on data analytics to navigate the ups and downs of the sales funnel. Analytics reveals the hurdles and accelerators by analyzing user interactions at each stage, from awareness to consideration and conversion.

Imagine a platform for online shopping that uses analytics to streamline the purchasing procedure. The platform can streamline payment alternatives or address security problems if data shows a large drop-off at the payment step. And what was the outcome? A more streamlined conversion procedure that grows the number of happy clients. The responsible use of this authority is of the utmost importance in the field of data analytics. A user's privacy is protected, and the journey through their data is conducted in accordance with legal and moral standards, thanks to the ethical compass. Establishing and maintaining trust between organizations and their audiences is achieved through transparent data gathering procedures, strong security measures, and compliance with data protection legislation.

Data analytics is like a conductor conducting a symphony of insights in the dynamic world of digital marketing. It's more than just looking at data and graphs; it's about understanding how users behave, trying to guess what they might need, and coming up with techniques that really connect with them. Data analytics acts as a compass for businesses, pointing them precisely and predictably toward success as they sail through the competitive waters. It's more than just a tool; it's the catalyst that changes numbers into wisdom, murky information into crystal clear understanding, and silent clicks into a climax of enthralling audience participation.

Romaine Morgan

- CHAPTER 3 -
CRAFTING COMPELLING CONTENT

Successful campaigns and strategies in the dynamic world of digital marketing now hinge on quality content. The vitality that it provides to businesses, their target consumers, and the development of brand identity and engagement make its significance incalculable. To make an impression in this day of information overload, when customers are inundated with signals from all directions, you need material that is both interesting and relevant.

Digital marketers place a premium on content because of its power to engage viewers on an emotional level. Digital marketing is defined by engagement and interaction, in contrast to traditional marketing, which relied on one-way communication. Content enables organizations to engage with their audience on a more personal and genuine level through blog entries, social media updates, films, and infographics. Through this exchange, a relationship beyond a simple transaction is formed, which in turn increases trust and loyalty to the brand.

Also highly valued by the internet's gatekeepers, search engines, is high-quality material. Search engines like Google use algorithms that are built to give consumers the most relevant, useful, and valuable content. Search engine rankings reflect this focus on high-quality information. Websites that have high-quality, relevant content have a better chance of ranking well in search engines, which increases their visibility and drives organic traffic. As a result, companies that put resources into making great content serve both their audience and search engines better. The content also has a significant impact on how people perceive and talk about a brand.

With so many options available to consumers online, a unique brand personality can help a company stand out. The brand's values, purpose, and USPs may be better articulated and reinforced through regular, high-quality content. Brands have the power to captivate their target audience and leave a lasting impression with video content, social media updates, blog entries, and other forms of digital storytelling.

Brands may now access a large and varied audience through the proliferation of social media platforms, which serve as potent distribution channels for content. Material with high levels of share-ability, relatability, and audience resonance has a greater chance of going viral, resulting in an exponential increase in its reach. In addition to demonstrating the efficacy of well-crafted content, this viral impact also provides a low-cost means of brand message amplification.

Making content that starts conversations and gets others to share it is important because social media algorithms also reward engaging material. When it comes to digital marketing, content is more than just words on a page. The use of visual elements, such as photos and videos, to attract and hold viewers' attention is becoming more and more crucial. Visually appealing content has a higher chance of being digested and remembered since the human brain processes visual information faster than words. Digital marketing campaigns that use a wide range of multimedia material allow brands to captivate consumers and build stronger relationships with them.

Content marketing is an approach that takes the long view, prioritizing relationship building and trust over quick sales. Businesses can establish themselves as leaders in their fields by giving helpful information, fixing problems, and meeting the demands of their target audience. Customers are more inclined to stick with a company they have faith in; thus, this positioning helps bring in new ones while keeping the ones they already have. To sum up, content is king when it comes to digital marketing. It is the engine that propels marketing success by engaging audiences, increasing brand awareness, and boosting search engine presence.

Those companies that put an emphasis on producing high-quality, relevant content will be the ones to stay afloat in the ever-changing digital market. The essence of successful digital marketing lies in narrative telling, value provision, and audience connection through multiple channels; content serves as the medium through which all of these things can be achieved. An engaging content strategy is like a tapestry: every thread is carefully selected to form a masterpiece that speaks to the audience.

Businesses may achieve their goals and build meaningful connections with their audience in the digital arena with the help of a well-planned content strategy. Information flows like a river in this realm. A writer's sensibility, an acute awareness of the reader, and a dedication to extraordinary storytelling are all necessary for this complex tango of words and meaning. Knowing your audience inside and out is crucial for developing effective content strategies.

A writer sets out on a quest to understand their audience on a deeper level, to find out what they want, what hurts them, and what they hope for. This investigation goes beyond simple demographics; it's an effort to understand the audience's inner workings and to hear their ideas and feelings. A content strategist, like a novelist, needs to make their audience feel something, whether it's through the characters they develop or the messages they convey.

A writer working in content strategy must establish the story's driving force before writing a word. Do you want people to learn something new, have fun, be inspired, or maybe even think deeply about something? It is critical to grasp the function of each piece of content within the bigger picture, since it is a chapter in the story. With this goal in mind, the writer may navigate the maze of ideas and make sure that everything fits together to form a coherent content strategy.

Building a consistent and smooth user experience begins with a well-thought-out content strategy. In order to take readers on a well-orchestrated journey, writers create roadmaps. Articles, videos, infographics, and social media updates all need to fit together like a symphony in order to captivate audiences across many platforms. A writer's skill with structure and timing is essential for this orchestration, which keeps the audience's attention from the first sentence all the way to the last call to action.

Consistency is the lifeblood of content strategy—the engine that keeps the story going. Similar to how a novelist keeps the same voice and style throughout a book, a content strategist needs to be consistent across all channels. No matter the tone of the piece—lighthearted social media or serious blog post—the readers should be able to detect the consistent rhythm. A consistent performance does not limit itself to playing just one note but rather incorporates a variety of styles that work together to create a beautiful whole. Content strategy is like a canvas painted with ink and colored with keywords— the language of the digital world.

The art of content planning requires a writer who can walk the fine line between being honest in their storytelling and using keywords for SEO. It's not about keyword stuffing, but rather about incorporating them naturally into the text so that search engines can see them. Keywords are more than just a tool; they are a vital part of the story and necessitate skill in this intricate dance.

A writer developing a content strategy for digital marketing, when attention spans are short, must harness the power of images.

Similar to how a writer uses words to create vivid scenes, a content strategy uses images to draw in viewers. Pictures and videos are like paintbrushes; they make the story come to life. Words without a visual symphony to enhance their emotional impact are insufficient, as any writer in the digital era knows. A content strategy is more like a living organism than a dry document; it changes and adapts as the digital world does.

As the content strategist keeps an eye on trends, analyzes data, and adjusts the story to remain relevant, their writing sensibilities come into play. The story is shaped by the audience's reactions, preferences, and shifting dynamics in an ongoing conversation that is always happening. Crafting a writer-infused content strategy is, at its core, an artistic pursuit, a symphony of words and ideas that rises above the ordinary and mesmerizes the reader. It's not enough to merely impart knowledge; one must also skillfully weave an emotional journey—an experience—that will stay with the audience forever. Content strategies are just marketing tools until they are crafted by a talented writer who elevates them to the level of art and a demonstration of the impact of storytelling in the digital era.

In the dynamic world of digital media, the art of captivating and compelling audiences to share material has emerged as a distinct discipline. Being able to create captivating and shareable content is a highly sought-after talent in today's information-overloaded environment. In order to create content that connects with readers and goes viral, writers in an ever-changing landscape need to have a firm grasp on the fine line between imagination and planning. Knowing your audience inside and out is crucial for creating engaging content. An accomplished writer knows their audience inside and out, understanding not just what they're interested in but also the feelings that motivate them to share.

It's important to consider not only the audience's wants but also their unanticipated desires. Finding unfulfilled needs and uncharted areas are great ways for writers to generate curiosity, which in turn increases the likelihood that readers will click the "share" button. Captivating headlines entice readers to delve further into the material. Headlines that are well-written entice readers by promising that what follows will be worthwhile. In addition to being brief and captivating, it should be easy to click on. Headlines are captivating because they can tease without spilling the beans. The skill of the tease lies in its ability to entice viewers to go further with just a few clicks or taps.

The meat of the piece is when the author's skills really shine. Presenting information in a way that engages and keeps the reader's attention is more important than just conveying it. A content creator's toolbox should always include storytelling, an age-old tradition. By building a story around the central idea, you may hook readers and create an emotional connection with them that goes beyond just exchanging facts.

In creating interesting information, visual components often take a back seat. The incorporation of captivating visuals, such as photos, infographics, or videos, can transform ordinary content into something truly captivating for humans. "A picture is worth a thousand words" is especially true in the digital world, where an appropriately selected image can express feelings and ideas that words alone would not be able to describe. Media integration not only makes the content more visually appealing, but it also makes it accessible to people with different learning styles, increasing its potential audience reach.

Engaging material is primarily about inventiveness, but relevancy is also crucial. For content to be shareable, its timeliness is paramount. Content is positioned as part of the ongoing debate when it taps into current trends, events, or cultural phenomena. In addition to making it more relatable, this boosts the possibility that readers will share it in an effort to add to the collective story. Rather than just watching the material, users are actively involved because of the interactive component. Inviting readers to take part in the conversation fosters a feeling of belonging, whether via polls, quizzes, or free-form inquiries.

Creating a community online may transform an infrequent sharer into an ardent fan of your company and a casual reader into an ardent follower in this era of ubiquitous connectivity. In the pursuit of shareable content, one must never discount the influence of emotions. What makes content more likely to be shared is its ability to evoke an emotional response, be it laughter, nostalgia, wonder, or empathy. Feelings establish an emotional bond, and it is this bond that elevates material from fleeting awareness to imprinted memory. If a writer can evoke strong feelings in their readers, their work will stay with them forever. Finally, there is a perfect synthesis of art and science in the production of interesting and shareable material.

It calls for an in-depth familiarity with the target demographic, storytelling prowess, excellent images, connection to the present conversation, interaction, and the capacity to stir up emotions. In the ever-growing digital world, where attention is more valuable than gold, a writer with these abilities can stand out from the crowd, get their writing recognized and shared, and eventually become a voice heard throughout the internet.

In the ever-changing world of content creation, where people's attention is valuable, using multimedia is crucial for captivating viewers and making a strong statement. Transforming static content into an engaging experience that connects with varied audiences is the goal of multimedia. This includes images, videos, infographics, and interactive elements.

Understanding the human preference for visual stimuli is fundamental to the successful integration of multimedia. Because of the inherent bias in our brains toward visual processing over text alone, multimedia is a powerful medium for conveying nuanced concepts and stirring up strong feelings. Visuals, when well selected, have the power to evoke feelings and ideas that words alone can't express, drawing viewers into the story on a deeper and more personal level. Pictures speak volumes in the digital world. Visuals, such as striking images or carefully crafted graphics, operate as an audience's initial point of contact with the material.

One must have an enticing image to pass the fabled "thumbnail test" and get viewers to click on to the full article. In addition to breaking up the monotony of text, pictures offer visual clues that boost comprehension and lead the reader on a journey. The narrative dimension that videos provide is what really draws in viewers and keeps them engaged because of how dynamic they are. Videos can captivate audiences with their storytelling and emotional depth, whether they're brief instructional clips, in-depth interviews, or visually breathtaking feature films. Video material is becoming more and more important in the multimedia arsenal, as seen by the popularity of sites such as TikTok and YouTube.

One of the most under-appreciated aspects of content comprehension is infographics. In today's information-overloaded world, infographics simplify complicated material into easily understandable visual representations. Infographics are visual representations of data that combine text, photos, and graphics to make the data more accessible and easy to grasp.

They are an effective means of clarifying complex ideas for the audience, increasing their retention, and facilitating their learning. Multimedia features that allow users to interact turn viewers into creators. Audience participation is encouraged through the use of interactive infographics, polls, and quizzes. This does double duty: it encourages engagement while simultaneously revealing useful information about the tastes and comprehension of the target audience. By introducing a two-way communication channel, the interactive dimension transforms the content from a monologue into a discussion. Although podcasts are mainly used for aural purposes, they can also be categorized as multimedia.

Words spoken aloud, accompanied by music or sound effects, can evoke strong emotional responses from audiences. A rising number of people are turning to podcasts as a means to get the information and entertainment they want on the go at their own pace. Incorporating multimedia components is a smart way to accommodate different learning styles and preferences; it's not just about making things seem better. Because different people process information in various ways, multimedia allows you to reach and engage more people.

A more significant and long-lasting effect can be achieved by connecting creators with their audience through this medium. Ultimately, when it comes to creating content for the digital era, multimedia components are essential. Multimedia components act as shareable engagement triggers by improving visual appeal and clearly communicating complicated ideas. Crafting content that not only informs but also leaves a lasting impact on the ever-evolving digital landscape requires carefully selecting photos, videos, infographics, and interactive elements in a world where competition for attention is severe.

Romaine Morgan

- CHAPTER 4 -
THE BASICS OF SEO

In the complex world of the internet, where websites compete for visitors' attention, knowing the fundamentals of SEO (search engine optimization) is like having a master key that opens all the doors to success. Search engine optimization (SEO) is like a map that helps companies and content creators navigate the complex maze of search engine algorithms in this dynamic and unpredictable online environment.

"Search Engine Optimization" (SEO) is more than just an acronym; it's an evolving approach to managing the myriad factors that influence a website's position in SERPs. Search engine optimization (SEO) is the practice of enhancing the visibility and usability of a website so that users are more likely to find and engage with the content therein. To better understand the internet, think of it as a huge marketplace where numerous stalls compete for customers' attention.

Search engine optimization (SEO) involves setting up shop at the crossroads where people are most likely to be walking. Before setting out on this digital adventure, it is essential to have a firm grasp of search engine optimization (SEO), the field where technological wizardry, content, and keywords come together to boost a website's visibility. The digital realm's money is keywords. People use these terms when they want to find a certain piece of information, product, or service online. You may converse fluently in search engine language by skillfully incorporating pertinent keywords into your article.

It's all about creating content like web pages, blog posts, and product descriptions that carefully use phrases that your audience is likely to search for. Use carefully chosen keywords that flow naturally through your content to guide search engines in classifying and ranking your pages. However, there is more to SEO than just using keywords wisely. When it comes to the internet, content is king. Virtual reality rests on three pillars: quality, relevance, and originality.

Think of your content as a lavish, interesting, and fulfilling meal spread out for your readers. In addition to being algorithms, search engines are like fine wine tasters; they can tell the difference between the extraordinary and the ordinary. Not only does this keep your material interesting and relevant, but it also shows search engines that your website is active and growing. But there's more to SEO than just getting your keywords and content to work together.

Technical dexterity is required. An optimized website is more than just a data warehouse; it's a well-oiled machine with a pleasant, intuitive interface. Improving page loading speed, making sure your site is mobile-responsive, and building a logical structure are all examples of technical SEO. An easy-to-navigate interface shows that you care about your visitors' happiness and sends a message to search engines that your site is trustworthy. Your familiarity with SEO will need to be updated when algorithms change. A never-ending conversation with the digital ether, a never-ending learning curve. Essential terms in search engine optimization include keeping an eye on statistics, understanding user behavior, and adjusting to new trends.

New algorithms and user behaviors appear like stars in the digital night sky; thus, successful navigation requires a vigilant eye on the horizon. The environment is dynamic. Backlinks are like the precious threads that tie your website's authority and trustworthiness into the vast web of search engine optimization. Digital endorsements in the form of backlinks occur when other websites indicate their agreement with your content's relevance and usefulness.

The wide breadth of the internet may be explored by search engines through backlinks, which are like a network of interconnected roads. A strong backlink profile is the result of persistent outreach, the cultivation of meaningful relationships, and the production of content that is so engaging that other people are eager to incorporate it into their online stories.

Finally, becoming familiar with SEO fundamentals is more than just a need; it's a ticket to the frontier of the internet. Making sure your web presence is in sync with the algorithms that control the flow of information in the digital era is the key. When people utilize search engine optimization (SEO), it acts as an unseen hand to lead them to the information, goods, and services they are looking for. The internet is a large and ever-expanding universe; to make your digital presence heard clearly and authoritatively in it, you must embrace its intricacies and nuances and begin a journey where you become fluent in their language.

In the complex world of the internet, where words have immense power, mastering the skill of keyword research and application becomes crucial for being seen online. The outcome of digital projects is decided by a language ballet that orchestrates the dance between user intent and search engine algorithms; it's more than just a strategic goal.

The internet is like a huge desert, and keywords are like elusive breadcrumbs that lead forlorn wanderers—your potential audience—to your digital shelter. Search engine query language can be deciphered using keyword research, which acts as a compass to identify trends in this breadcrumb path. In the ethereal world of the Internet, it is crucial to comprehend the cadence of your audience's queries. To start, you need to put yourself in the shoes of the person you're trying to help or provide a temporary reprieve from. Discovering these digital traces is the skill of keyword research, which entails mining the language of your intended audience.

How do they communicate with the empty space of search boxes? As they seek knowledge or amusement, what phrases are on the tips of their fingers as they type? In this linguistic dig, tools like SEMrush and Google's Keyword Planner serve as metaphorical shovels and pickaxes. They reveal not only words but also the core of intent, the hidden wants, and the questions included in user input. It's not enough to only find popular keywords; you also need to hear the delicate rhythm that distinguishes a casual browser from a serious seeker and decipher their searches accordingly.

Now that we have this lexical treasure trove, the next step is to put it into action. Instead of being ornamental, keywords are the threads that make up the digital fabric you design. Like a skilled chef delicately blending a dish with a symphony of tastes, the secret is seamless integration. Without detracting from the overall flow of the story, every keyword serves its purpose. Search engine crawlers and readers alike will remember the integration as a graceful dance, a choreography in which keywords waltz their way through your paragraphs. The point is not to overstuff text with keywords but rather to subtly incorporate them so that they support the story without coming across as inauthentic.

The mantra is strategic placement. Keywords provide a vivid image for both human readers and algorithmic scrutinizers in your content's titles, meta descriptions, headers, and body. It's all about finding that sweet spot where your content's core ideas stay true while keywords boost its visibility in the huge online echo chamber. Still, words don't conclude the symphony. This digital composition includes visual components like photographs and movies as notes.

You may enhance the multimedia experience and make your digital work more discoverable by using alt text, captions, and file names as extra canvases for keyword brushstrokes. Consistent improvement is the curtain call on SEO's vast stage, where algorithms serve as critical actors. Changes in user behavior and keyword trends are constants on the ever-evolving digital stage. You may keep your digital performance in sync with the ever-changing dynamics of the virtual audience by conducting regular audits and making tweaks to your keyword approach.

This will serve as your continuing rehearsal. To sum up, researching and implementing keywords are not just technicalities; they are the poetic lyrics that enhance your digital story. It's the skill of creating a mutually beneficial interaction between algorithms and users that goes beyond the limitations of coding. Keywords are more than simply a string of characters; they are the melodies that reverberate through the internet's virtual halls, leading seekers to the treasures you have painstakingly laid out in your virtual refuge. Keep this in mind as you negotiate this complex dance.

Romaine Morgan

- CHAPTER 5 -
PAY-PER-CLICK ADS

As the world of digital marketing is always changing, companies are always looking for new ways to reach their customers and make an impact. To satisfy this need, pay-per-Click (PPC) advertising has become an effective strategy.

Paid search (PPC) advertising has become an essential tool for companies seeking to increase their online presence, lead generation, and revenue due to its low cost and high dynamic range. Basic pay-per-click (PPC) advertising is the practice of charging a fee to the advertiser whenever their internet ad is clicked. Here, companies can bid on terms that are relevant to their target audience through an auction-based approach. The advertisements are shown prominently when people use these terms on search engines or while browsing websites.

The performance-based strategy is crucial since it only pays advertising when users click on their ads. Google Ads, the undisputed leader in the search engine industry, is the go-to platform for pay-per-click advertising. Ads on Bing, Facebook, and Twitter are among the most popular platforms. Advertisers can modify their campaigns to reach their target demographic by making use of the individual features, targeting choices, and ad formats offered by each platform.

Instantaneous results are one of the main benefits of pay-per-click advertising. Search engine optimization (SEO) and other organic tactics take months to yield results, but pay-per-click (PPC) advertising can reach the top of SERPs nearly instantly after campaign launch. Businesses seeking to swiftly launch an online presence or advertise time-sensitive deals must prioritize this instant visibility.

Pay-per-click advertising lets businesses zero in on certain demographics, geographic regions, and even device types. Advertisements are shown to users with a higher likelihood of interest in the advertised products or services with this level of specificity. By maximizing the efficiency of ad expenditure, businesses can reach the right audience with the right message at the right time by refining targeting settings. Businesses are given more budgetary leeway with PPC advertising.

Advertisers have more control over their expenditures when they set daily or monthly budgets. Businesses can also modify their offers in response to performance and market demand through the auction-based bidding system. With this leeway, companies may maximize the return on investment (ROI) of their advertising budgets. The measurable nature of pay-per-click advertising is one of its distinguishing aspects.

Detailed analytics and reporting are provided by PPC platforms, in contrast to more conventional types of advertising, where it can be difficult to measure return on investment. Advertisers may monitor important metrics such as clicks, impressions, and conversions, which enables them to make decisions based on data. Because of this openness, companies can improve their tactics, find the keywords that work best, and tweak their ads until they achieve optimal performance. Display ads on social media sites like Facebook and Instagram are an example of pay-per-click (PPC) advertising's expansion outside search engines.

This is a great way for companies to reach their target demographic with eye-catching advertisements, which helps to build brand recognition. Advertisements for pay-per-click services are highly adaptable and successful since they include both text and visual components. The scalability and adaptability of PPC advertising are unparalleled.

Changing targeting criteria, experimenting with new creatives, or adjusting ad copy are all things that advertisers can do in real time to improve their campaigns. Businesses that are nimble enough to react quickly to shifts in the market, seize new opportunities as they arise, and maintain a competitive edge are able to thrive. In addition, it is simple to increase the size of a successful campaign in order to reach more people or enter new markets.

One of the most important aspects of digital marketing is pay-per-click advertising, which provides firms with a versatile and effective tool to reach their online objectives. Businesses of all sizes can benefit from pay-per-click advertising due to its rapid results, targeted advertising, flexible budgeting, guaranteed measurable return on investment, increased brand exposure, adaptability, and scalability. Adopting the strategic advantages of pay-per-click (PPC) advertising is becoming more of a need for individuals who want to succeed in the cutthroat online marketplace as the digital ecosystem keeps changing.

You have entered the exciting and ever-changing realm of internet advertising, where success is at your fingertips! Get ready for some mind-blowing digital marketing wins because I'm about to spill the beans on how to set up and manage Pay Per Click (PPC) campaigns. Imagine this: You have an excellent service or product, but how can you get the word out to the people who will really benefit from it? That's when pay-per-click (PPC) ads come in like digital superheroes, making sure your brand is seen all over the world.

Let's take your company to the next level by embarking on this thrilling adventure together. Like creating a masterpiece, setting up a pay-per-click campaign calls for meticulous planning, imaginative execution, and a dash of strategic genius. Locate your intended readers with pinpoint accuracy. So, who could end up buying from you? Could you tell me what they like? With this information in hand, we create captivating advertisements that speak to your target demographic, pique their interest, and inspire them to take action.

In pay-per-click advertising, keywords are king, and we can show you how to mine them for gold. We connect your business with people who are actively searching for what you provide by conducting thorough keyword research to identify the terms that reverberate through the digital halls. Placing your advertising in great digital real estate strategically without breaking the bank becomes an art form when you master bid management. Ad creatives are the meat and potatoes of your pay-per-click campaign, so let's get into them now. We design experiences, not just advertisements. Captivating headlines, convincing text, and striking images—each component is a stroke on the customer engagement canvas.

What is our objective? So that your ad can be seen clearly among the many others on the internet. However, it is just the beginning of our adventure; now we must plunge into the exciting realm of optimization and analytics. In order to drive our ongoing process of improvement, our cutting-edge tools analyze campaign results and provide valuable insights.

We spare no effort in our pursuit of PPC perfection, whether it's modifying bids or honing ad wording. We are the master choreographers, making sure every step of a pay-per-click campaign goes off without a hitch. In order to stay ahead of the competition, our team is dedicated to tracking trends, adjusting strategy, and more.

Your campaign will not only survive but thrive because we use real-time data to make adjustments and pivots. Conversions, brand exposure, and a remarkable return on investment are more important metrics in pay-per-click (PPC) advertising than clicks alone. Are you prepared to take your online presence to the next level, attract qualified visitors, and see your company thrive? Join me on this exciting PPC journey, where each click brings us one step closer to victory! Budgeting and bidding tactics are the building blocks of digital success in Pay Per Click (PPC) advertising, which you are about to enter.

Maximizing your return on investment (ROI) and catapulting your brand to the forefront of the digital frontier require mastery of these tactics in the lightning-fast realm of internet advertising. Budgeting is the first step because it provides the necessary funds for any pay-per-click campaign. If your budget is like a canvas, then every click is like a brilliant stroke. You must first determine how much money will be spent on various campaigns, ad groups, and keywords before you begin.

Regardless of the size of your budget, we strive to help you get the most out of every dollar. The adaptability of PPC is its greatest asset. You can exert pinpoint control over expenditures with the use of daily, monthly, or campaign-specific budgets. Whether your campaign's goal is to increase brand recognition, generate leads, or close deals directly, we can adjust your budget to meet your needs. In response to the ever-changing nature of online customer activity, our budgeting solutions are designed to be dynamic. As a PPC campaign's lifeblood, let's talk about bidding now.

Platforms like Google Ads require a deliberate approach to bidding due to their auction-based nature. We explore the complex realm of keyword bidding, zeroing in on the sweet spot for maximum efficiency while simultaneously striving for first place. By utilizing automated bidding algorithms and other smart bidding tactics, we can tap into the potential of machine learning to optimize bids to their fullest extent.

When it comes to bidding, quality score is our best-kept secret. We boost your quality score by improving the relevancy of your ads, the experience of your landing pages, and your click-through rates. This will allow you to pay less per click and have higher ad placements. The dance is intricate and needs precision, and we will guide you through it.

When it comes to successful bidding tactics, ad extensions are often overlooked. Your ad's exposure and click-through rates will both increase thanks to these extra bits of information that give users more incentive to click on it. We will carefully use technologies like site link extensions and callout extensions to make your ad stand out and make it more effective than the competition.

Data is king in pay-per-click (PPC) marketing. We use powerful analytics technologies to get insights and make smart decisions. In order to remain ahead of the competition, we constantly track and analyze performance indicators. This allows us to identify keywords that are performing well, modify our bids appropriately, and enhance our strategy.

Bidding and budgeting for pay-per-click campaigns require a mix of planning, research, and flexibility. We're not merely handling campaigns; we're composing a digital masterwork that connects with your target demographic and propels your company to new heights of success.

Are you prepared to see how strategic bidding and budgeting may revolutionize your business? We can help you become a digital marketing master by enhancing your PPC strategy.

Romaine Morgan

- CHAPTER 6 -
ANALYSIS

Data has become the backbone of effective marketing tactics in the ever-changing digital era. There is no way to emphasize the significance of data in determining marketing campaigns as companies move from analog to digital platforms. Staying competitive and relevant in this era of unprecedented connectivity and information flow requires leveraging data.

The essay delves into the significance of data in digital marketing and how it powers targeted advertising and informed decision-making. The ability of data to offer insights into customer behavior is one of the main reasons for its tremendous importance in digital marketing. Analyzing the data points generated by every click, scroll, and interaction on digital platforms can reveal trends, preferences, and patterns. Marketers can gain a detailed understanding of their target audience with the help of this abundance of data, which in turn allows for the development of highly targeted and personalized campaigns.

Businesses can better target their audiences with relevant marketing campaigns by using data analytics technologies to learn about consumer tastes, internet habits, and needs. In addition to shedding light on customer habits, data also gives marketers the tools they need to quantify and assess the success of their initiatives. Marketing campaigns can be fine-tuned by tracking key performance indicators (KPIs) like engagement metrics, conversion rates, and click-through rates.

Businesses may better use their resources with this data-driven strategy, putting money into tactics that pay off in the long run and cutting ties with those that don't. Agility allows marketers to respond swiftly to shifting customer tastes and market conditions by measuring and analyzing campaign results in real-time. Improving the customer journey also relies heavily on data.

It is critical to understand the customer journey along the sales funnel in light of the abundance of digital touch-points. Through the analysis of user interactions across many channels, companies may pinpoint problems, obstacles, and opportunities for enhancement.

Marketers may use this information to improve the customer journey from the first point of awareness all the way to the final conversion. Customers are more likely to be loyal to a brand, make repeat purchases, and spread the word about their excellent experience when they have a smooth and tailored journey. In addition, hyper-targeted advertising has entered a new age with the advent of big data. Using data to generate highly personalized and pertinent content has allowed marketers to move away from using generic, one-size-fits-all campaigns.

Businesses can reach out to certain demographics with personalized messaging by using data segmentation and targeting. This way, each audience segment receives material that speaks to their own tastes and requirements. By reducing ad spend on irrelevant populations, this level of targeting not only improves the efficacy of marketing activities, but it also helps to save money. When it comes to social media marketing, data is also king. Social media sites like Twitter, Instagram, and Facebook offer marketers a wealth of data about their audiences, including demographics, engagement rates, and the effectiveness of their content.

With this data in hand, companies can hone their social media tactics, provide more engaging content, and fine-tune their advertising campaigns. By utilizing social media listening technologies, companies can keep tabs on what people are saying about their company, products, or industry online. This data is extremely useful for shaping marketing campaigns and determining where to place the brand.

The value of data in online advertising is crucial, to conclude. The foundation of modern marketing strategies is data, which helps with analyzing consumer behavior, measuring campaign effectiveness, refining the customer journey, and enabling hyper-targeted advertising. In today's fast-paced and information-rich digital world, companies that can effectively use data to their advantage will not just make it through but thrive. Businesses must adopt a data-driven strategy to remain competitive in the digital marketing landscape, where data will play an increasingly important role in influencing future trends as technology progresses.

Romaine Morgan

- CONCLUSION -

Being able to quickly adjust to new circumstances is an absolute must in the dynamic world of digital marketing. Changes in consumer habits, new algorithms, and lightning-fast technological developments characterize this ever-evolving marketplace. In order to succeed in this competitive landscape, marketers need to highlight how digital marketing is constantly changing and encourage a mindset of continuous learning and adaptability.

With the rise of new technology, digital marketing has expanded far beyond its traditional boundaries. The digital marketing scene is being transformed by a myriad of factors, including social media, AI, data analytics, and augmented reality. Both the opportunities and the complexity of marketing have grown with the advent of these instruments.

Recognizing the ever-changing nature of the market and actively seeking out ways to enhance one's skills are crucial for professionals to remain competitive. The ever-changing habits of consumers are a major force propelling the rapid evolution of digital marketing. The proliferation of digital marketing channels is directly proportional to the pervasiveness of technology in people's daily lives. If you want your marketing efforts to be successful, you need to understand these changes in customer behavior. Marketers have responded to the proliferation of mobile browsing by creating content specifically for mobile devices and adopting a mobile-first strategy.

To satisfy a customer base that is always on the go, these adjustments are necessary. Also, the foundation of internet visibility—search engine algorithms—is always changing. Marketers need to keep up with the ever-changing search engine algorithms if they want to keep their online presence strong and attract more customers.

Marketers need to stay updated on search engine optimization trends to make sure their content is discoverable. Yesterday's strategies might not work today. Analytics is crucial in determining marketing tactics in the era of big data. On the other hand, data analysis tools and methodologies are always improving. Marketers need strong data interpretation skills to get useful insights for making decisions. As new technologies and approaches come out, it is essential to regularly refresh foundational skills like understanding key performance indicators (KPIs) and exploiting analytics tools. Marketers may adjust their strategy and get demonstrable results by continuously learning data analytics.

Digital marketers must prioritize lifelong learning if they want to thrive; doing so will also spur innovation. Opportunities for marketers to test out new ideas, try out new technology, and lead the way in developing trends are presented by the industry's fast pace of change. Organizations can encourage innovation in digital marketing by creating an environment where employees are encouraged to ask questions and learn new things. It is essential for digital marketing teams to prioritize professional growth. This might manifest in a variety of ways, such as taking advantage of online education opportunities like classes and certificates or going to relevant conferences and webinars.

Staff members' skill sets and the team's overall knowledge base are both enriched when leaders promote a culture of lifelong learning. Team members that are knowledgeable about current developments in the sector and can offer different viewpoints make cross-functional collaboration more effective. To sum up, in today's ever-changing digital world, success hinges on recognizing the fluidity of digital marketing and fostering a culture of continuous learning and adaptability. What differentiates successful digital marketers is their capacity to adjust to new technologies, comprehend changing customer habits, and anticipate algorithmic alterations.

Experts and businesses can succeed in today's digital marketing environment by adopting a growth mentality, which allows them to learn new things constantly and adapt to changing market conditions. Success in the ever-evolving field of digital marketing will go to individuals who aren't afraid of change and who make learning their top priority.

Romaine Morgan

- OTHER BOOKS TO CHECK OUT -

Milton Keynes UK
Ingram Content Group UK Ltd.
UKHW051951301123
433416UK00023B/969